UNCOMMON WOMEN

Laura Winters

Uncommon Women: Explorers

Scobre Educational
42982 Osgood Road
Fremont, CA 94539

www.scobre.com
info@scobre.com

Scobre Educational publications may be purchased for
educational, business, or sales promotional use.

Cover design by Sara Radka
Layout design by Nikki Ramsay
Edited by Jennifer Skogen and Lauren Dupuis-Perez
Copyedited by Malia Green
Images sourced from iStock, Shutterstock, Newscom, and Alamy

ISBN: 978-1-62920-588-5 (hardcover)
ISBN: 978-1-62920-587-8 (eBook)

table of contents

SACAGAWEA 5

WHEN LONDON IS NOT ENOUGH 13

"THE ICE WOMAN" 19

WOMEN MUST TRY 25

THE VIEW FROM UP HERE 31

THE DEATH TRAIL.. 37

THE BLUE PLANET 41

GLOSSARY 46

BIBLIOGRAPHY 47

Lewis and Clark, the two leaders of The Corps of Discovery, and Sacagawea are immortalized in this statute at Fort Benton, Montana.

Chapter One
SACAGAWEA

In 1806, in the mountains of present-day Montana, men of the Shoshone tribe saw a group of nearly three-dozen white men walking on Shoshone territory. Suspecting the white men to be a war party, the Shoshone raced toward them on horseback. Suddenly, a young Shoshone woman stepped out from the group of white men. The Shoshone men saw that the woman was carrying a baby. The Shoshone slowed their horses, moving with caution and curiosity toward the woman. Her name was Sacagawea, and she was a translator, a mother, and one of the first modern female explorers.

Two years earlier, United States President Thomas Jefferson needed men to explore and map the 827,000 square miles of land purchased from the French. U.S.

DID YOU KNOW?

The Louisiana Purchase doubled the size of the United States. The land cost $15 million, or mere pennies an acre.

Captain Meriwether Lewis and Second Lieutenant William Clark were chosen to lead this expedition. Lewis, Clark, and the other male volunteers were part of a group called The Corps of Discovery.

The Corps set off on their journey with books, scientific instruments, and weapons. What they did not have was someone who could speak the languages of

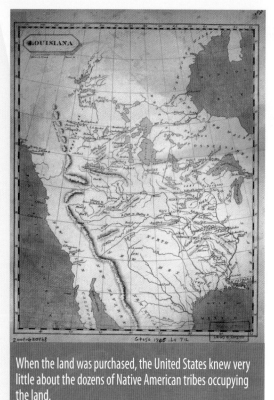

When the land was purchased, the United States knew very little about the dozens of Native American tribes occupying the land.

the Native American tribes living in the newly acquired lands. This need for an interpreter would lead them to a young Shoshone woman, Sacagawea.

Sacagawea was born around 1788 in Lemhi Country, Idaho. She grew up traveling the area's trails through forests of tall, skinny trees, and swimming in small veins of larger rivers. She was the daughter of a Shoshone chief, and had a brother named Cameahwait. Aside from where she was born, not much is known about Sacagawea's childhood.

An attack from the Hidatsa, an enemy tribe, brought Sacagawea's peaceful childhood to an end. The Hidatsa raided the Shoshone and stole Sacagawea from her home. They carried her east into their territory, to what is now North Dakota.

After being kidnapped, Sacagawea and another Shoshone girl were sold to a French-Canadian trapper named Toussaint Charbonneau who lived among the Hidatsa. Charbonneau made both girls his wives. Sacagawea was, at most, 13 years old, and Charbonneau was about 33.

Sacagawea, Charbonneau, and his other wife lived together for four years until the Corps arrived. The Corps waited out the winter in the Hidatsa-Manda villages. There, they met Charbonneau and asked if he and Sacagawea would join the expedition. Charbonneau would be paid for his work, but Sacagawea would not. As was the 19th-century custom, Sacagawea went along with her husband's decision, and she became the only woman on the expedition. Her role was crucial to Lewis and Clark's success.

The Corps needed four different members who spoke four different languages in order to speak to the Native Americans.

Without computers or phones, translating took a chain of people who could speak multiple languages. To speak to the Shoshone Tribe, Lewis and Clark would speak to Corps member Private Francois Labiche in English, who would speak to Charbonneau in French, who would speak to Sacagawea in the Hidatsa's language, who would speak to the Shoshone in their native language.

When the Corps headed west in April, Sacagawea performed her translating duties whenever necessary. She also noted landmarks and paths. She knew which plants and berries were poisonous and which would feed the hungry travelers. And she did it all while caring for her infant son, Jean Baptiste. Sacagawea often proved to be even more useful than her husband.

Lewis described Charbonneau as "perhaps the most timid waterman in the world," and said that he was "a man of no peculiar merit." Charbonneau earned these descriptions after nearly sinking the Corps' boat . . . twice. Both times, Charbonneau was standing in for the **helmsman**, and when Charbonneau was faced with great winds and waves, he ended up turning the boat the wrong way.

In May of 1805, during one of Charbonneau's mishaps, the boat filled with water. The maps, journals, and reports of the Corps began to float away. Sacagawea stood calmly on the deck and snatched pieces of paper and journals before they washed over the side of the boat, saving Lewis and Clark's carefully recorded discoveries.

For the Corps to reach the Pacific coast, they needed to cross the Rocky Mountains. Sacagawea and the Corps faced all the dangers modern hikers face: avalanches, storms, freezing temperatures, scalding sun, and mountain lions. The big difference was that they didn't have any of the modern tools that today's hikers have. The safest, fastest way to cross was on horseback. Charbonneau assured Lewis and Clark that Sacagawea would be able to secure horses from the Shoshone.

Sacagawea was the Corps' greatest hope for crossing the Rocky Mountains safely.

This was Sacagawea's first return to her homeland since being kidnapped. In an incredible coincidence, the Corps encountered a tribe led by Cameahwait, Sacagawea's brother. The two reunited happily, and she convinced Cameahwait to sell horses to the expedition. But the Corps could not linger with Sacagawea's family for very long. No one knows exactly why Sacagawea continued with Lewis and Clark. Maybe she enjoyed being a useful part of the expedition, maybe she wanted to keep her son close to his father, or maybe she never questioned that she must obey Charbonneau's plan to finish the journey with the Corps to receive his pay. Whatever the reason, Sacagawea left her brother and her people to cross the Rockies with the Corps. She would never see Cameahwait again.

DID YOU KNOW?

After reaching Oregon, Lewis and Clark asked each of the Corps members to cast their vote on where they should stay the winter. As a trusted member of the group, Sacagawea was allowed to vote as well.

On November 15, 1805, after successfully crossing the Rocky Mountains, the Corps reached the Pacific Ocean. The group spent the winter near the ocean, and then travelled back east to bring their findings to President Jefferson. In total, the Corps walked 8,000 miles over two years. Once the trip was finished, Sacagawea and Charbonneau travelled from state to state as Charbonneau looked for work, eventually settling in South Dakota. Sacagawea gave birth to a baby girl named Lisette in August of 1812. After childbirth, Sacagawea fell ill with "putrid fever" and died in December of the same year. She was around 24 years old.

Sacagawea died before anyone outside of the Corps of Discovery learned of her accomplishments. Over the next few decades, relationships with the Native Americans and white settlers dissolved into suspicion, hatred, and eventually many battles. It wasn't until Eva Emery Dye published *Conquest: The True Story of Lewis and Clark* in 1902 that Sacagawea came into the public's attention. In an attempt to bolster the importance of the one woman on the expedition, Dye exaggerated Sacagawea's accomplishments. But the stories about a Shoshone woman helping two white explorers captured America's imagination, and Sacagawea became the subject of numerous plays, movies, poems, and statues. In 2000, the United States government honored Sacagawea's contribution to America by placing her image on the golden dollar.

Sacagawea is the second woman to have her image placed on money. Susan B. Anthony appeared on the first dollar coin in 1979.

When Mary became an orphan, she received money and opportunities that were unheard of for women of this era.

Chapter Two
WHEN LONDON IS NOT ENOUGH

In 1872, 10-year-old Mary Kingsley was in her family home of Islington, England, curled up in her father's library. While a small fortune was spent to educate Mary's brother Charles, school was considered unnecessary for Victorian girls. So, Mary made do with her father's travel journals. With Charles at school, her mother sick in bed, and her father doing research in America, Mary could read her father's writings with little supervision. She especially enjoyed the unfinished journal with sketches of Africa, a country so different than England—and 6,000 miles away.

Mary spent most of her childhood and early adult years caring for her parents, who were often ill. When they died, Mary inherited £4,300, a sum worth over $400,000 today. She decided to spend her inheritance money traveling to Africa. Some say she chose Africa because she hoped to complete her father's unfinished journals.

Mary wrote to missionaries and to the English outposts in Africa to tell them of her impending arrival. She outfitted her trunks and bags with nets, tubes,

DID YOU KNOW?

In the 1870s England controlled India, Australia, Canada, and parts of Africa. It was said that the sun never set on the British Empire.

Mary's first stop on her African travels was Sierra Leone.

journals, and other means of collecting and recording wildlife. By August of 1893, Mary was ready to set sail. It was considered improper for an unmarried woman to travel without any sort of chaperone or companion. Mary knew that she was breaking many Victorian rules just by stepping aboard.

She reached Freetown in Sierra Leone, and climbed off the ship wearing her iconic outfit: full mourning black for her parents, and a daring red silk tie. As she set foot on the sandy shore, her dull Islington life vanished. She was off to encounter things no British woman—and very few British men—had ever seen before.

Among the many groups of Africans she met, Mary insisted on meeting a West African cannibal tribe, the Fan or Fangs. In her later speeches and books, Mary shocked Europeans by recounting the pleasant time she had with the cannibals. She taught them a few words of English and exchanged goods. Mary described the cannibals as "full of fire, temper, intelligence and go."

Mary also drew constantly, and wrote about many plants and animals on her trip. She had the thrill of finding a new species of fish, whose Latin name "Ctenopomoa Kingsleyae" ensures no one can forget the Ms. Mary Kingsley who discovered it.

Mary also became the first European woman to reach West Africa's highest peak, the 13,255-foot summit of Mount Cameroon. As Mary and a small support team climbed upwards, attendant after attendant decided not to continue on the ascent. Only Mary and one other person reached the highest point, and they were rewarded for their efforts. They saw acres of trees on rolling grounds and, as Mary wrote, the "white gauze-like mist comes down the upper mountain towards us: creeping, twining round and streaming through the moss-covered tree columns" (*Travels in West Africa*).

Although Mary was thrilled to see the beauty of West Africa, she also became familiar with its dangers. Europeans had nicknamed Africa the "White Man's Grave" because many of the Europeans who went to visit never came back. Most of the Europeans were killed by diseases they had never encountered back home. These travelers

DID YOU KNOW?

Victorian women wore dresses over corsets and petticoats. Despite the difficulties skirts could cause while exploring, Mary said she would rather "perish on a public scaffold" than wear pants.

faced swarms of mosquitos and sandflies carrying **malaria**. Mary also encountered large predators like crocodiles and leopards.

On one hot and humid day, Mary and her attendants were canoeing down the Ogowe river. The 90-degree day made Mary's long black sleeves and heavy skirts uncomfortable. Her paddle rippled the murky water, and Mary paused to wipe her brow under her netted hat. The other end of her canoe jerked suddenly, dipping into the water. Mary gasped as a massive crocodile emerged from the water, trying to pull itself into the small boat. Remaining calm as the beast advanced, Mary gave the crocodile "a clip on the snout with a paddle," and the crocodile shimmied back into the water.

After her first trip, Mary could not be kept from Africa, and made two separate, year-long trips in 1893 and 1894. Her travels had been well-reported in the United Kingdom and she was invited to give lectures at the Scottish and Liverpool Geographical Societies. Because it was rare for women to give public speeches in front of male audiences, Mary sat on the stage while men read her books for her. During her nationwide speaking engagements, Mary gained the confidence to tell her own story. She was the first woman to address the Liverpool and Manchester Chamber of Commerce.

In Mary's opinion, British colonial rule forced West Africans to believe in daily and religious customs that were not practical for the region. For example, while Christian Missionaries were trying to convince the West Africans that a man should marry one woman instead

of many, Mary insisted that a single wife would not be able to clean and feed an entire household.

Mary enjoyed her success in England, but was determined to return to West Africa. She set sail in 1900 but landed in Cape Town, South Africa instead of West Africa. In Cape Town she served as a nurse in the Boer War, a war between the United Kingdom and an African territory that wanted to be free of British rule. As a nurse, she served British prisoners of war, trying to combat a nasty wave of **Typhoid** fever that had swept through the Boer's trenches. Within weeks, Mary caught Typhoid and died. Her death distressed those in England. "With all the go and independence of the New Woman she embodied the sterling qualities of the Old Woman—humility, love of home and family, and a simplicity of nature which was truly refreshing" (*The Graphic*, "The Late Mary Kingsley"). At her request, the great explorer was buried in the waters that stretched between England and Africa, the country she loved at birth, and the country she grew to love until her death.

Louise not only appreciated polar bears from afar, but sometimes took part in polar bear hunting expeditions.

UNCOM

Chapter Three
"THE ICE WOMAN"

The deep green lake lay smooth and undisturbed. A polar bear slept in the weak sunlight. Then, far-off thunder rumbled, and grew loud enough to stir the polar bear from her nap. There was something large and metal shooting through the sky. It was 68-year-old Louise "Ice Woman" Arner Boyd and her pilot, in a private plane. Louise became the first woman to fly over the North Pole in 1955. After 40 years of northern exploration, this trip would be her last expedition into the arctic.

Louise was born in 1887 to parents who had made a fortune in the **Bodie Gold Rush** in California. But money could not keep the family from tragedy. Both of Louise's brothers died of rheumatic fever at 16 and 17 years old. In the early 20th century, it would have been far more traditional for Louise's brothers to carry on Mr. Boyd's business; but finding himself without sons, Lousie's father made 22-year-old Louise the president and manager of Boyd Investment Company. He also sent her to **finishing school**, and gave Louise her first camera.

Tragedy struck Louise again when

DID YOU KNOW?
A brand new Kodak camera cost about $25 at the turn of the century, or $600 today.

explorer

Witnessing the natural wonder of Polar Ice reshaped Louise's future.

both her parents died in 1920. Louise was the sole inheritor of the family fortune. However, she grew bored throwing lavish parties and redecorating her home, and she turned her efforts to traveling and photographing Europe.

While on a boat to Norway in 1924, Louise fell in love with a new photography subject that would consume the rest of her life. Wrapped in thick furs, she exited her cabin and climbed the narrow steps to the deck. The frigid wind whipped at her face as she staggered to the boat's railing. She looked out and saw her first Polar Ice Pack: miles of thick, unbroken ice, gleaming in the cold sunlight. Louise looked at the ship's captain standing next to her, then looked across the frozen sea and said, "Someday, I'm going to be in there, looking out, rather than out here, looking in."

In 1928, Louise made good on her promise to be "in there." Pilot Roald Amundsen was missing in Norway, and Louise lent her chartered boat *The Hobby* to the search effort on one condition: that she be allowed on the journey. For three months, the crew searched for Amundsen over 10,000 miles of ocean. She took 20,000 feet of film footage, and thousands of pictures. Her photographs captured the hard realities of life on a ship, as well as breathtaking

views of glaciers and late sunsets. Amundsen was never found, but the King of Norway awarded Louise the Chevalier Cross of the Order of Saint Olav for her generosity and courage. She was only the third woman in the world to receive this honor, and the first American woman.

In 1931, Louise planned a new expedition for herself, this time to explore and photograph the **fjords** of Greenland's east coast. She made multiple trips over three years and took pictures of all the fjords between the King Oscar Fjords and the Franz Josef Fjords. With her eye toward the landscape, Louise and her crew noticed something: a passageway between two fjords that was on no map. She led her crew down the unexplored passageway. Greenland rewarded her bravery by naming its inner fjords "Miss Boyd Land."

Louise proved that the North was more than a rich woman's pet project. She became known as an accomplished scientist and photographer who took half a dozen trips north between 1933 and 1941. The American Geographic Society sponsored Louise to photograph even more fjords. The U.S. government paid for her to return to Greenland in 1941 to study the effects of the north pole

explorer

on radio communication.

During World War II, Louise was the first woman to volunteer her service as a military intelligence consultant on matters of the North, particularly Greenland. Louise requested the salary of only one dollar a year. Louise celebrated with the United States when World War II ended, but her work was not done. She needed to see the North Pole, which would be the crown jewel in her explorations.

At 68, she achieved that goal. In her article "A View from 9,000 Feet" (Parade Magazine, 1958), Louise wrote, "North, north, north we flew. Soon we left all land behind us . . . and as I saw the ocean change to massive fields of solid white, my heart leaped up. I knew we were approaching my goal. Then— in a moment of happiness, which I shall never forget—our instruments told me we were there. […] My Arctic dream had come true."

Her accomplishments did not end with the Arctic. The University of California, Berkely, awarded her with an honorary law degree. She became the first woman elected to the American Geographic Society board in 1960. The California Academy of Science gave her an honorary membership. Between paying for her expeditions and bad investments, Louise lost most of her money by the end of her life and had to sell her home in San Rafael. She died on September 14, 1972.

Louise was 68 when she achieved her Arctic dream.

Amelia saved up money for months to buy her first plane.

Chapter Four
WOMEN MUST TRY

Twenty-year-old Amelia Earhart had never been that impressed with airplanes, until her friend dragged her to a stunt-flying exhibition. Amelia stood in the field with the rest of the crowd, waiting for the pilots to do their tricks. A sudden roar meant a show plane had taken off. The pilot spotted Amelia and her friend, who were huddled together, and swooped right toward them. Amelia's friend screamed and backed away but Amelia stood her ground. She stared back at the pilot as he pulled up the plane and shot back into the air. From that moment on Amelia "knew [she] had to fly."

This knowledge had to wait as she finished high school and entered finishing school. She dropped out of finishing school to become a nurse aid in World War I. After the war, Amelia took flying lessons from a pioneer female aviator named Anita Snook. Amelia loved every moment—the speed, the freedom—and instantly wanted her own plane. After saving for months, she bought a bright yellow two-seater she called "The Canary." On October 22, 1922, Amelia and her Canary shot 14,000 feet into the air, a new female altitude record. This was seven

DID YOU KNOW?
Amelia was born on July 24, 1897, in Atchison, Kansas.

explorers

months before she became the 16th woman to be issued a pilot's license.

Amelia was an unknown pilot in 1928 when pilot and publicity coordinator Captain Hilton H. Railey asked her to join a crew flying over the Atlantic. Three other crew members had died attempting to become the first woman to complete the journey, but Amelia was up for the challenge.

On June 27, 1928, she and her co-pilots took off from Newfoundland. Amelia and the two men checked their instruments, fixed mechanical problems, and kept each other awake. Twenty-one hours after take-off, the crew landed in Wales as heroes. They returned to the United States, met President Calvin Coolidge, and marched in a parade thrown in their honor.

After her flight from Newfoundland to Wales, Londoners welcome Amelia Earhart.

Amelia was not satisfied with gaining stardom through this flight. "Stultz did all the flying—had to. I was just baggage, like a sack of potatoes. Maybe someday I'll try it alone." And four years later, after planning with her husband and publicist George Putman, Amelia became the first woman to fly solo across the Atlantic.

Ignoring those who said the trip was too dangerous, Amelia climbed into her plane on May 20, 1932. The wind was rough and blowing north as she started up her engine in Harbor Grace, Newfoundland. She waved goodbye, and tore into the sky. She fought winds and icy conditions the entire time. Near the end of her trip, weather conditions worsened and the plane began to experience mechanical difficulties.

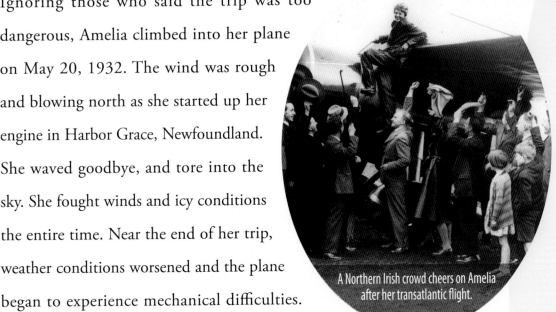

A Northern Irish crowd cheers on Amelia after her transatlantic flight.

Although her plan was to land in Paris, Amelia would need to make an emergency landing if she was going to live. She came down through the clouds, spotted a pasture, and landed. She climbed out of the airplane not in Paris, but on a farm in Northern Ireland—tired, but ecstatic that she had set a new record.

Amelia's nickname "Lady Lindy" came from the world-famous male pilot Charles Lindbergh. But Amelia was much more than a female version of Lindbergh. She set a new altitude record of 18,415 feet that went unbroken for years. She was the first person to make a solo journey from Hawaii to California. She was the first person to fly from Mexico City to Newark. She became the first star to design and promote a clothing line at a department store.

After her cross-Atlantic success, Amelia wanted to go further. She wanted to prove that a female pilot could make it all the way around the world. On July 7, 1937, Amelia and her navigator Fred Noonan settled into Amelia's Lockheed Electra plane. The pair had sectioned off their journey around the equator into more than two dozen smaller trips. California to Arizona, Venezuela to Suriname, Chad to Sudan. Around the world she flew, traveling 22,000 miles in less than two months. On July 2, Amelia and Fred left Lae, New Guinea, and headed toward their next stop: Howard Island. The pair never arrived.

When Amelia was declared officially missing, the United States government shot into action, spending four million dollars on the most expensive sea and air search of that era. After 11 days without results, the United States reluctantly called off the search. To this day, there have been many theories about Amelia's fate, but no one knows exactly what happened.

Amelia's spirit remains in the letters she wrote to George during her around-the-globe journey. In one such letter, Amelia wrote, "Please know I am quite aware of the hazards. [...] I want to do it because I want to do it. Women must try to do things as men have tried. When they fail their failure must be but a challenge to others."

Amelia Earhart stands with Paul Maas, Harry Manning, and Fred Noonan in front of her Lockheed Electra airplane at Honolulu Airport, Hawaii, on March 20, 1937.

Valentina started her path to becoming
a cosmonaut with parachute jumping.

Chapter Five

THE VIEW FROM UP HERE

Valentina Vladimirovna Tereshkova was born to peasants in the town of Maslennikovo, Russia, in 1937. At 18, Valentina joined her mother working in a textile mill. She joined the Young Communist League, and after becoming a full member of the Communist Party, she gained access to the Yaroslavl Air Sports Club. While at the Sports Club, the 22 year old began parachute jumping. She loved the thrill of the wind rushing through her hair and the earth rushing toward her feet.

It was her practice with parachutes that made Valentina a perfect candidate for the Soviet space program. In the 1960s, **cosmonauts** were expected to jump out of an aircraft 20,000 feet in the air and parachute to earth on the return journey from space. Already an **exemplary** Communist and secretary of her local Young Communist League, Valentina volunteered for the Soviet space program. The Space program accepted her for training because of her 120+ parachute jumps, and she fit the physical requirements. A cosmonaut needed to be under 30 years of age,

DID YOU KNOW?

Although the United States and the USSR fought as allies in World War II, the tension between the political theories of capitalism and communism made the two superpowers enemies during The Cold War.

Valentina used the Vostok spacecraft simulator to prepare for her mission.

under 5'6" tall, and under 154 pounds.

Valentina and four other women trained for 18 months and endured a variety of tests. She spent days alone to see how she handled isolation. She was placed in a human centrifuge, a machine that spins people, to see how her body would handle rocket take-off. Valentina endured a heat chamber, multiple parachute jumps, and took a flight in an MiG-15 jet that could go high enough out of the Earth's atmosphere for Valentina to experience weightlessness.

It was down to two Valentinas to see who would be the first woman in space. Valentina P. had tested better, but she smoked, took unescorted trips, and when asked, "What do you want from life?" she responded, "I want to take everything it can offer." Valentina Tereshkova answered, "I want to support irrevocably the […] Communist Party." Valentina Tereshkova got the job.

On June 16, 1963, the 26-year-old Valentina became the 12th person to travel into space on the Vostok 6. As the larger rockets fell off and she was pushed outside of the Earth's atmosphere, Valentina was captivated by the unending darkness, and the distant, glimmering stars.

Inside the Vostok, things were not so

DID YOU KNOW?

The United States and the USSR were competing in a scientific space race to get the first man on the moon. The U.S. won that race on July 20, 1969, when Neil Armstrong set foot on the moon.

awe-inspiring. Valentina's cabin was only 7.5 feet wide. Her instructions were to stay strapped in her seat to avoid sickness, and to perform a few scientific tasks for one single day of flight. But Valentina noticed an error in the spacecraft's landing calculations and was forced to stay in space while ground control sorted out the issue. Strapped in one position for three days, she had no additional tasks to complete in the extra time. Her right ankle throbbed and her helmet pressed painfully on her shoulders. She developed a rash under her suit.

Valentina's shuttle was small and uncomfortable.

By the time the landing calculations were corrected and Valentina could return to Earth, she had orbited 48 times in three days. The amount of time she spent in space was longer than all of the American astronauts combined.

In her return, she ejected herself from the Vostok 4.3 miles from the ground even though her parachute would only open at 2.5 miles. She free-fell, then opened her parachute, narrowly avoiding water as she landed. Her face was badly bruised in the fall. Due to the space race with the United States, and a desire to keep up Soviet Union morale, it was very important to the USSR that Valentina's trip be perceived as a flawless triumph. During the press conference about her flight, Valentina wore make-up to cover up her bruises, and avoided discussing all the discomforts she experienced in space.

After her successful mission, Valentina became a USSR hero.

For her accomplishments in space, Valentina received the Order of Lenin and the Gold Star Medal. Back on Earth, she became a spokesperson for the Soviet Union and received the United Nations Gold Medal of Peace. She served in a variety of political positions, including the Supreme Soviet of the Soviet Union, the highest legislative body in the Soviet Union. Even after the collapse of the Soviet Union, Valentina remained a respected hero. In 2008, she began her role as deputy chair of the Yaroslavl parliament. Now in her late 70s, Valentina is a living part of cosmonaut history.

Junko fell in love with hiking as a child, and set her sights on climbing Everest as an adult.

Chapter Six

THE DEATH TRAIL

Mount Everest is the tallest mountain in the world, and the deadliest. More than 200 people have died while attempting to reach the highest summit. At 5.5 miles above sea level, a climber can be killed from lack of oxygen, from severe cold, or a single slip of the foot. None of these dangers kept Junko Tabei from reaching the summit.

Junko was born in Japan in 1939, and climbed her first mountain at age 10. She attended Showa Women's University and studied English literature. While her studies did not focus on the outdoors, Junko was pulled back to the mountains she fell in love with as a child.

After she graduated college, she founded the Ladies Climbing Club in 1969. Her club set its sights on Everest after looking at each of the world's mountain ranges. They picked Everest because they could read the journals and notes of those who had climbed Everest before, and plan accordingly.

After the club picked Everest, Junko acted against the traditions of polite Japanese culture in the 1970s. She left her three-year-old daughter with her

DID YOU KNOW?

On May 29, 1953, Edmund Hillary and his Nepalese Sherpa, Tenzing Norgay, became the first two climbers to ever reach the summit.

husband in order to climb the perilous mountain. "Back in 1970s Japan, it was still widely considered that men were the ones to work outside and women would stay at home. [...] Even women who had jobs—they were asked just to serve tea" (Japan Times). Junko planned to do more than serve tea.

On May 16, 1975, Junko and her **Sherpa** guide, Ang Tshering, pulled themselves onto the South Summit of Mount Everest. Other women in Junko's club remained at a base below. Junko and Ang were 28,750 feet above sea level, but they had more than 300 feet to go before they reached the top. Junko sat in the snow and caught her breath. She spotted a piece of the mountain she had not been prepared for: a perilous knife ridge. A knife ridge is a very thin stretch of rock, this one on a downward slope, 50 feet long, and covered in ice. "I had no idea I would have to face that, even though I'd read all the accounts of previous expeditions. I got so angry at the previous climbers who hadn't warned me about that knife-edge traverse in their expedition records," Junko said in a post-climb interview.

The South Summit of Everest is especially perilous.

Junko pushed her anger aside and focused on her dream of reaching the top.

She lowered herself into the snow, got on her hands and knees and crawled sideways along the thin rock. This ice ridge runs along the border of two countries, Nepal and China. As Junko scooted across the rock, her upper body was in China and her lower body in Nepal. She moved slowly. She breathed slowly. If she slipped, she had miles to fall.

Junko waved a Japanese flag when she reached the top of Everest.

Junko reached the end of the ridge. She was relieved, but she and Ang still had some distance to climb. Her legs and arms ached from fighting against the snow and ice, and her breath was shallow. But upward she went until she reached the summit. She became the first woman to ever do so.

Junko, literally on top of the world, stood and waved her Japanese flag, nothing behind her but clouds and snow.

Junko's Everest achievement sent her in search of other mountains to conquer. By 1992, she was the first woman to reach the highest peak on each of the seven continents. She wants to climb a mountain in every country on the planet. With climbs achieved in 60 countries, the 77 year old only has 136 more countries and mountains to go.

Dr. Sylvia Earle fell in love
with the ocean at age 13.

Chapter Seven

THE BLUE PLANET

Dr. Sylvia Earle was born in 1935 on a farm in New Jersey. She was not exposed to the ocean until her family moved to Florida when she was 13. The ocean called to her and she immediately took up scuba diving as a hobby. By 1966, Sylvia was beginning groundbreaking work in **botany**, oceanography, and marine biology with her dissertation at Duke. Her work *Phaeophyta of the Eastern Gulf of Mexico* was the most complete first-person account of aquatic plant life ever written. Dr. Earle has made categorizing every aquatic plant life in the Gulf of Mexico one of her life-long projects.

Unfortunately, Dr. Earle's intelligence and accomplishments could not overcome the **sexism** of the 1960s. Sylvia applied for a position in a project that would send four scientists to the Tektite habitat, an enclosed dome 50 feet underwater, for eight weeks. She had logged more diving hours than any male applicant, but was refused a position in the project. Sylvia said, "The people in charge just couldn't cope with the idea of men and women living together underwater."

DID YOU KNOW?

Tektite I was completed by four men. They lived underwater for 58 days.

In response to being turned away from the first underwater mission, Sylvia organized a team of leading female scientists to inhabit Tektite. The women were studying the effects on humans of living in an enclosed, underwater space, as well as how fish respond to shadows, and how fish use grass to hide from predators. The Tektite base was a NASA project, therefore Sylvia's Tektite mission was the first NASA mission to have an all-female crew. When the scientists emerged from the sea, they were greeted with a parade and a visit to the White House.

Sylvia followed sperm whales around the world.

In the 1970s, Sylvia went everywhere the water did—to Galapagos, to the water off Panama, to China and the Bahamas, and to the Indian Ocean. She followed sperm whales around the world from Hawaii to New Zealand, Australia, South Africa, Bermuda and Alaska.

In 1979, Sylvia earned the nickname "Her Deepness" by setting the world record for the deepest dive without a tether back to the surface. At noon on September 19, she waded into the Pacific ocean's warm water and checked that her equipment was working. She wore a Jim Suit, a pressurized metal suit protecting Sylvia from the pressure of 600 pounds per square inch, which she would encounter at

The Jim Suit was an essential component to underwater exploration.

a quarter-mile below the sea. Sylvia and the tiny submarine lowered into the water. The water grew cooler as Sylvia plunged into what she described as the "twilight zone, where sunlight fades and darkness begins to take over. [...] A thousand feet and below, it is truly dark."

At 1,250 feet, a quarter-mile below sea level, Sylvia was tethered only to the small submarine. She is the only human to conquer such depth without being tethered to land. In an interview with radio host Krista Tippet, Sylvia described what happened when she had the submarine turn off its headlights. When the ship's lights went dark, she saw "the flash and sparkle and glow of bioluminescent creatures." She witnessed corals that, when touched, "little rings of blue fire pulsed all the way down from where I touched to the base of these spiraling creatures. They were taller than I." Sylvia spent two and half hours on the ocean floor, about the same amount of time that the first astronauts spent on the moon.

Today, Dr. Earle wants others to experience deep dives. She started two companies that design underwater vehicles for the sole purpose of helping scientists reach the ocean depths. She also led the Google Advisory Council on creating Google Maps for the ocean. Currently, Sylvia heads Mission Blue, a project that works to create marine protected areas, like forest preserves, for the ocean. Mission Blue has created 50 "Hope Spots" of protected ocean, and is working to create more.

Sylvia was enchanted by the bioluminescent coral. This coral glows when agitated.

GLOSSARY

Bodie Gold Rush: from 1877 to the mid-1880s, the town of Bodie, California, saw a huge population boom after the discovery of gold

botany: the study of plant biology

cosmonauts: Russian astronauts

exemplary: the best example of something

finishing school: a school attended by young women, usually of the upper class, that would teach them proper manners

fjords: long, narrow strips of ocean between two high cliffs

helmsman: the person who steers a boat

malaria: a deadly disease caused by tiny parasites living on mosquitoes

numerous: many, a large amount

sexism: prejudice or dislike based on gender

Sherpa: a group of people in Tibet who live high in the Himalayas; many work as guides to mountain-climbers looking to climb Mount Everest

typhoid: a disease caused by a bacterial infection involving a high fever

BIBLIOGRAPHY

The Journals of the Lewis and Clark Expedition. 2005. U of Nebraska Press / U of Nebraska-Lincoln Libraries-Electronic Text Center.

Amelia Earhart, "The Official Website." http://www.ameliaearhart.com/

"Demystifying Mary Kingsley." Jacqueline Banerjee, PhD, Associate Editor, the Victorian Web. www.victorianweb.org/history/explorers

"Women of the Polar Archives: The Films and Stories of Marie Peary Stafford and Louise Boyd." National Archives: Prologue Magazine. Summer 2010, Vol. 42, No 2.

"Valentina Tereshkova". Encyclopædia Britannica. Encyclopædia Britannica Online. Encyclopædia Britannica Inc., 2016. Web. 25 May. 2016

"Junko Tabei." Everest History. http://www.everesthistory.com/tabei.htm

"Sylvia Earle: Oceanographer." The National Geographic.

"Transcript for Sylvia Earle - Her Deepness." O Being with Krista Tippett. June 7th 2012.

explorer